SCR  THE FACADE

If you just opened this book while sitting
on the pot, here's a hint;

Just flip to any random page and enjoy.

SCREW
THE
FACADE

Self Love
(without the messy cleanup)

by James Ewing
www.screwthefacade.com

A STF Publishing Book

ISBN--13: 9780692646618
ISBN-10: 0692646612

FORWARD

By Kelly Marceau, founder of "Sexy. Conscious. Awake."

When I met James, I appreciated his commitment toward his personal development while simultaneously embracing his wild humanity. Often times when it comes to self-realization humans limit themselves by thinking they have to choose one or the other. Some nonsense around thinking that being one-dimensional is superior to the messy dualistic nature of humanity. If humanity would just embrace the truth that we are a little messed up but that most of us take life way too effing seriously, we'd appreciate the multidimensional reality of our beings who can be all shades of sloppy and classy, even in the same night!

The guy who is trying to be someone he's not, trying to be what he thinks people want so that he will be seen as someone important, is boring and painfully predictable. The guy who is recklessly human but owning his shit and still having a good time while evolving, now that is real.

Thank you, James, for keepin' it real. For not being afraid to download this cosmic joke and wonderful saga called life.

KM

GRATITUDE

Special thanks to my Dad, for teaching me about the power of God, spirituality, healing, truthfulness, and most importantly, love. I love you Dad, and I'm sorry in advance for the course language in this book. *(maybe Mom can read it to you and bleep out the bad parts?)*

So much thanks to you, Mom, for encouraging me that I can do anything and be anything that I desire to be. For instilling in me a huge faith in humanity, and forgiving me of all my craziness. Thanks for believing in me. I love you.

Thank you to Misti Davis, for holding up a mirror for me while we journeyed together in our relationship. You showed me what it looked like to know me fully, with all my flaws and eccentricities, and love the shit out of me. Had you not shown me unconditional love so fully, it would have taken me much longer to learn to love <u>myself</u> unconditionally. I'm glad we're still friends. ☺

To LeAnne Steen, Chad Shields, Todd Gaughan, my brother Dr. John, my best friends John and Hayley, my ex-wife and ex-girlfriends with whom I've loved and grown so much. Thanks for putting up with my crazy antics while I was still asleep, or just waking up, and thank you for forgiving my relentless pursuit of self-development.

Thank you to the countless other friends who've not only have taught me so much but also told me over and over again that they believe in me. I am blessed to know each and every one of you.

Thank you to Kelly Marceau, my coach and mentor, for using your gifts to guide me to a place where I could discover, own, and love my shadow self. You are one-of-a-kind in this world and I'm so glad I hired you way back then.

Thank you to all my other coaches and mentors along the way. Thanks to Dan Merideth who taught me the value of not giving a shit whether people like you or not in business. Thank you David Deida for teaching me about polarity and Kyle Cease for teaching me to 'just start'. Thank you to Anthony Robbins and Wayne Dyer for inspiring me so many years ago.

I love you all, James Ewing.

Introduction

This book is definitely not for everyone. I wrote this to share my humanity: the good the bad and the ugly as I have journeyed on this path to owning my true self. To the few who are on the cusp of awakening, you'll love the sh** out of it.

When I first sat down to write this it was a letter to my younger self. I did not intend to publish it, and when that changed I most certainly did not intend to use my real name. Somewhere along the way, however, I found myself. Weird, isn't it, that while writing a letter to my younger self that I'd end up falling in love with my current self?

Yet – that's what happened.

I started coaching when I was very young, although I didn't know that's what it was called. I called it ministry (I used to be VERY religious). I love people, always have, and if I can help someone have a better day I make every attempt to do so. I also have a knack for seeing the future in technology, making good money, and empathizing with others at a deep, intuitive level. What I did not have throughout my life, however, was self-love.

As I wrote the letter to my younger self I found some gems along the way. First, I discovered I've learned a ton. Second, I discovered that on a percentage basis, whenever I was alone, I was actually kinda sad, and often seriously depressed.

I had all this head knowledge, good health, great friends, and from the outside looking in,

I had a wonderful life. In reality though, I was wearing a mask. A mask that made me look like I was a badass, even though I didn't feel like one. I'm pretty sure the majority of people that came to the shows while I was the singer for Tone (my old band) thought I was living *the life*. I had my married friends coming by asking me about whatever girls I'd met over the last month, and they would tell me they were living vicariously through me.

Yet – I was lonely. I was depressed.

I was living a façade.

My marriage hadn't made me happy. My success in business hadn't made me happy. My success as a wakeboarder, songwriter, lover, none of it made me truly happy. Happiness and peace were eluding me.

I found the hard truth very slowly.

I needed to love myself in order to be truly happy.

That's when I changed the book (a little) and decided to publish it under my real name. So – here ya go. ☺

This is not a book to read cover-to-cover. The goal, in truth, is that you'll leave a copy in your guest bathroom for those times when someone needs the right kind of wisdom. And, they'll find it because ... well, because that's just how the universe works.

So, flip to a page and enjoy.

Oh, and one more note...

This book is intentionally designed to be a book to read while you're dropping the kids off in the pool, so I imagine it will be present on the bare legs of many a man and woman.

The thought, actually, of a fine female holding my book between her bare legs and laughing while peeing makes me smile immensely.

Happy reading - and I hope everything comes out OK.

SELF-LOVE

(Without the messy cleanup)

"[People] don't really mean what they say, they just got their own issues and what-not. All's I gotta do is keep bein' a good person, no matter what, 'an good things 'ill come my way. Everything's gonna happen for me, just as long as I never have no in my heart."

Joe Dirt

We all have this deep desire to be seen, understood, liked, admired, and maybe even envied. We want to be thought of as smart and sexy. Have you ever thought about why this is?

The answer: **we crave love**.

We desperately desire to be loved, by others, by ourselves.

The most challenging aspect of this craving, however, is to love ourselves exactly as we are and where we are.

In this work, I've learned that I have three parts to me: Body, Mind, and Spirit. Additionally, I have three parts to my mind / brain. This is called a triune brain.

The oldest and most unintelligent part of me is the limbic region (or lizard brain). It's where the unconscious memories of deep emotions are stored and experienced.

The middle portion is my mammalian brain (all mammals have this). My subconscious operates mostly from here.

The smartest part of my mind, however, is in the frontal lobe (the neocortex). This is the part of me that is aware that I exist, that can ask the question "who am I" and "why am I on this planet?"

The foundation of Screw The Façade is this: Learn the truth about who you are. Not who society or your parents wants you to be. You. The original you, the you that you were before you *didn't* get your emotional needs met or someone hurt you or made you feel you weren't enough just by being yourself.

If you don't know this, I'm telling you now:

You were formed and now exist as a result of, and as a part of, pure love.

This love isn't of the hallmark variety, it's your source, the essence of what makes you feel endless joy and appreciation for those moments in life that take your breath away or make you laugh your face off to the point it hurts. Love is the most powerful of all emotions and the opposite of fear, and you belong to it and it belongs to you.

14

Did you know your balls float when you're in the bathtub? Try it.

You're welcome.

There's a huge difference between people who have their shit together and know it, and everyone else in the world. The difference is a perspective, a mindset, a state of being. When you're connected to your own internal love, you automatically bring good shit into your life and to those around you.

Feeling bad today? Just get out of your own head, listen to your body tell you what you need, and **always remember that the hamster in your head is crazy** - and that truth is only found when you look (and listen) below your neck.

There's something intrinsically spiritual about good sex - which is why it's called making love.

Regardless of gender,
Femininity is freedom, craving presence,
Masculinity is presence, craving freedom.

We need each other to experience this, which is why jerking off isn't even close to the same thing.

Making love connects a man in his masculine to the divine feminine energy that is in nature.

I've recently discovered a fundamental truth about God. First off – I believe God created humanity so that he can experience what it's like to be in a physical body, through us, and with us.

As pure spirit, we can't experience physicality without our bodies, but our bodies have no awareness on their own.

Now, think about this for a minute, if He created us as part of Him, then He shares a spiritual connection with us. When we're connected to our souls, God is connected to us. So, the best gift you can give yourself and God is to strengthen and enjoy the connection you have with your own soul.

All those desires you have that you think you "shouldn't have"…? Yeah – that's B.S. God created you – and therefore - you're perfect

– even with all those desires. It's your ability to choose whether to act on them or not and then the results of those choices that become your gifts to the world.

Those desires you've repressed, shoved under the rug, pretended you don't have because you think you 'shouldn't' have them? Those desires are called your **shadow self**. Until you acknowledge them and love them as part of you, they will eat away at the connection you have with your soul and with God.

To connect with them, meditate (just sit for a while without judging your thoughts). PS: If you're like me you might need Brain.FM to do this at first.

Advice from my dad: If you're taking a dump in the wilderness, test the branch you're planning on holding yourself up with before you drop your drawers.

Dad, I feel kinda bad sharing that story without asking you first, and sorry about the rash on your butt that week in the middle of the Gila wilderness (why'd you pick a cliff again???). But (no pun intended), you handled it like a man and taught me the value of being tough (you're the toughest man I've ever known). You taught me how to enjoy life even when you're physically uncomfortable. Thank you, it's served me well over the years and I'll never forget it.

Getting out of our own way is something I've heard many a writer prose, yet they don't often explain how the hell to do it. The answer is simple - love is within you, in your body, in your heart, and the thoughts in your head are the barrier to love. Love is the opposite of fear, and when you realize that, you'll find that fear is what keeps you from discovering that deep inside you lives pure love, and a desire to give it unconditionally.

How strange is it then, that when we think about love, we automatically focus on what we think we must do or be to deserve it?!!!

You already are love - you already have it, there's actually nothing to chase.

I recently went on a date with a beautiful woman who told me she was fat about six times during the date. She wasn't fat - at all - but there's not a damn thing I can do or say to convince her of this. It was a complete turnoff (seriously – I didn't even want to have sex with her . . . ok, that's not totally true, I'd have loved to have sex with her, but it was still a turnoff).

Bottom line - your attitude is more important than your physical attributes - EVERY - FRICKIN - TIME.

When you're in a relationship and the other person get's angry with you for something you said, remember that only 40 percent of their emotional state is your responsibility. There's a whole lot more going on in your partner and situations like this can be a great opportunity to learn about him/her.

The key here is emotional intelligence. We all need to feel safe in order to grow (remember that a lobster needs a rock to feel safe enough to shed his shell and grow). If you defend yourself, you are removing your partner's ability to feel safe. So – don't defend, inquire and show them you really want to understand more about them. This is what's called "holding space" for your partner.

There's a conundrum that most young men find themselves in at least once in their life. It's when you meet your girlfriend's mom or sister and find her sexually stimulating. You try desperately to figure out how to be cordial and nice, but in the back of your mind you're trying not to hit on her. Here's a hint: Don't say, "Damn, your mom is hot".

You're welcome.

Loving yourself is what Screw The Façade is all about. It's not easy. I know this first hand. Here's how I did it;

1. Get to know yourself as you are today and remember that who you think you are presently isn't the same you that existed yesterday or last year.

2. Embrace your dark side (AKA shadow self) and do not judge yourself for having those desires. You can still have them, and now that they're acknowledged they'll quiet down a bit.

3. Abandon the dogma of your youth. Choose what YOU believe based on you – not your parents, family, or society.

4. Know that you'll change; we all do, and don't be afraid of it.

5. Take the time to sit in silence (some call it meditating) and let the thoughts

in your head pass through without judging them.

6. Always remember that you are born of love, and that you're connected to everyone (even me). When you don't seem to know the answers in your head, stop looking there and listen to your gut, where God and everyone else on the planet (who, by the way, desires the best for all of us) lives.

7. Study and learn from those you respect (like me!)

8. If you find yourself hitting a wall (sometimes a wall to your heart, which is an old self-protection mechanism) don't stress. Take some time, feel it all the way through, and if you need help, ask for it (from a good coach, mentor, or healer).

In every interaction with kids, always say something slightly inappropriate. This way you'll never have to babysit. Here's a hint: "Hey there, little Johny, how are you? Did you poop yet today?"

You're welcome.

If you've ever had someone tell you to just 'be yourself' and thought – well how the heck do I do that? Then you're not alone.

The reason for this is that you have four versions of you.

1. The you that everyone else sees
2. The you that you think everyone else sees
3. The you that you think you are
4. The real you, deep down, that's connected to love / God / the universe.

My advise is to find the 'you #4' and be that version of you all the time. This is what the person who loved you meant when they said, "Just Be Yourself".

As I grow older I get less and less judgmental, especially when it comes to judging myself. Allowing myself time to grieve without telling myself some BS like 'Pull yourself together man!' is awesome.

When you realize that deep within you is a force much bigger than you are, that wants the best for you, so that you can offer your best to the world and help change it; you'll find that giving yourself time, space, and allowing screw-ups without thinking of them as screw-ups is frickin' awesome. So...live it up, screw-up, it's all part of the journey. ☺

Men and women together:
what a glorious mess.

Roman Ramsey

You **can** have too many friends. If this happens then your focus get's diluted and your friendships will turn into acquaintances. Choose your close friends, therefore, just like you choose the razor you use on your private parts. It's that important.

In the dance between masculine and feminine, the biggest sexual attraction doesn't come from similarity it comes from **polarity**. Polarity is the 'opposites attract' side of things.

Now, I'm not a fan of relationships where you don't have compatibility (you need a huge amount of that), but you also need some differences in order to keep the sex drive high and the sheets moist.

In a sexual relationship you need one person who is more of a thinker AND is the leader, and the other person who is more of a feeler AND ok with being a follower (I call it 'allower'). It doesn't matter which gender is which, as long as both people aren't fighting for the same role. I call this "Thinking/Feeling, Leading/Allowing".[i]

If you ever get pulled over or arrested, just remember that cops are people too. They have their own struggles and shit that they have to deal with, and today you're the shit they're dealing with. Make it easy on them and they'll be easier on you (my apologies, by the way, if you're reading this on the shitter while in prison).

Lots of people will only travel with their friends or girlfriend.

This is stupid, especially if you're a guy.

You SHOULD travel by yourself. You'll meet people who would never have talked to you if you weren't alone.

At some point in every person's life they will find themselves feeling powerless over their attraction to another person.   When it happens, remember this:

Underneath that beautiful exterior is a person with a beautiful soul, just like you.

Our genetic programming makes them seem irresistible, but remember that you are more than a lizard or a mammal, **you have a triune brain** (triune = three parts working together). Your neocortex allows you to choose whether to follow your mammalian instincts or not.

Do this:

1. Use your neocortex to get rational and remember he/she is only human
2. Remember that you're totally unique
3. Remember that you are pure love, and interact at that level - because that that's all that really counts

One of the best investments I've ever made was Lasik for my eyesight.

Worth every penny.

Dad, I remember that day when I said I was going to get Lasik (20 years ago) and it was $1200.00 and you questioned it. I didn't have the understanding I do today. I think you were worried I was prioritizing my money over my wife and (future) family and it worried you. Well, I totally respect that view now, but I'm so glad I did it. Love you dad.

Have you ever had 'splash-back' while taking a dump? It's much worse in a port-a-potty. Here's how to fix that problem. Pull off about 5 feet of toilet paper and drop it in the port-a-potty first, then, Bomb's AWAY! No splash and easy cleanup of your good ole bum cheeks.

You're welcome.

True love

=

Desiring for your partner's highest spiritual growth above all else, including your own interests.

There's this huge movement today in young people, it's a quest for enlightenment, happiness, and connection. I believe the reason for this is that people feel a shift. The younger and less jaded you are, the more likely you are to feel the pressure of this shift.

The shift is a move to return to love, to heal others and heal our planet - and it comes with the intuitive knowledge that the fat lady's going to sing if we don't.

Polarity attracts two people and as a byproduct makes them want to have sex. It's the yin and the yang of masculine/feminine, alpha/beta, and thinking/feeling that makes sex hot. Most relationships will have a reduction in polarity (and therefore a reduction in hot sex) after a time since both partners begin to think and behave more and more like their partner.

This loss of polarity can be reversed: First have the alpha/thinker in the relationship begin to take control (even to the point of dominating the beta/allowing partner in the bedroom).

If you're the alpha/thinker, stop using the phrase, 'I dunno, where do YOU wanna eat?'.

Spark comes right back. You're welcome.

In today's relationships love is a misunderstood word. I love my friends, I love all of humanity, I even love you although I've not met you yet. When it comes to relationships, however, I think of it kind of like the word fuck. It's an adjective, a verb - a myriad of different things. Some folks underuse it, and some folks overuse it. Be in the middle;

Say "I love fucking you" before you say "I fucking love you" because it'll mean more when the receiver knows you know the difference.

Rules for guys when interacting with women:

1. When you're walking next to her on the sidewalk, always walk on the street side
2. Open doors – it's a sign of respect for yourself and for her
3. Pay for dinner, if she offers to pay, politely decline. If she asks you out, still offer to pay, but at that point if she says she wants to pay, then accept it as a gift
4. Do not EVER call a woman a cunt or a slut, even when you're around only men. Keep love in mind, however, that the men who degrade women with their language have suffered in their past; so have compassion on them
5. Start her car for her on cold mornings so it's warm when she gets in
6. Once in a while take her car and fill it up with gas or wash it so she won't have to

The best sex occurs when two people are connecting to one another at a spiritual level. The physical act isn't actually the breast part (see what I did there?).

If you're a man and you're only worried about performing well (making sure she has an orgasm) then you're doing it wrong.

If you're a woman and you're worried about looking sexy instead of just embracing the moment, then you're doing it wrong.

You'll know when you're doing it right when time stops...you forget who you are and what you're doing, and you end up relishing every scent, texture, sound, and movement. It will transcend the physical and become a spiritual thing. THAT's good sex. That's making love – and it won't matter if the lights are on or not.

The thing that's eluding most people about finding love is that they don't understand that love is a choice. Whether you choose it unconsciously, semi-consciously, or consciously, you are choosing someone based upon what you feel you are worth. Don't enter into a committed relationship with a low sense of self-worth. If you do then you are choosing to wake up the hard way.

My advice: discard the rules and boundaries that traditional relationships in today's society impose upon you and your partner, instead, choose to love them every day, and enjoy it when they choose you every day.

"Excuse me, is that corn in your hair?   'Cause you're the shit!"

Life isn't like a box of chocolates, sorry Forest. It's more like a box of motion-activated firecrackers with the occasional stick of dynamite in there. The whole, 'you'll never know what you're gonna get' bit is a lovely piece of advice, but hoping for the future can have the negative repercussions of not fully enjoying the present.

Far better to put your energy into loving the people who are in your life NOW than to wait for 'someday', which in reality may never show up.

You are here for a reason - whether you realize it yet or not - and that reason isn't to just show up and vote, its way bigger than that.

Take the time to figure out why you're on this planet, then live it.

This is called the "Art of Fulfillment".

You'll live a happier, more fulfilled life when you live a life with purpose.

Have you noticed people getting better looking with each generation? This isn't 'cause you're getting older. Each generation **is** better looking than the previous, genetically this has been happening for centuries, but we're past the tipping point. Stunners abound, and you're not left behind, as a matter of fact the best realization to take home is that the gene pool we're all swimming in is getting cleaner, clearer, and more fun. Enjoy it - don't envy it.

One of the most valuable tools I've learned along the way came from Byron Katie in "The Work". It helped me out of depression, and I still use it today. It goes like this:

1. Find a thought that's bothering you, (it helps if it includes the word "should" or "shouldn't".)
2. Ask, "Is this true?"
3. Ask, "Is this really true?"
4. Ask, "Can I absolutely know it's true?"
5. Ask, "Who would I be without that thought?"

If you get stuck – look up 'the work' on YouTube or buy her book.

As I get older some of the things I used to do easily aren't as easy anymore. This is normal, and eventually you'll be ok with it. In the meantime just find new stuff to do that you like, after all, that's what life's about anyway.

At the edge of every morning awakening, you'll find that an erection erases most of the memory of any dream you had the night before. This is caused by blood rushing to your penis to compensate for an overly full bladder. When the blood goes down south, you're brain freezes up due to low blood pressure.

This is why most men can't speak in the morning and simply roll over and hope she's somehow magically naked, interested, and already moist.

We all have humanity in common, but what makes a person great isn't what they have in common with others, it's what makes them different.

Ever feel different than everyone else around you? GOOD! Hang on to that, be weird, amplify that part of you and live it to the fullest. This is what makes you great at being you, great at life, and great at love.

After a long day of working, I like to sit on the back porch, sometimes with a drink or a bowl, and just sit there quietly. When my girl comes out to tell me about her day, I always smile and say "I'm in my ritual, come join me." Then I hand her the herb or a drink and hope she doesn't talk.

When inevitably she starts talking I say "Shhh . . . shhh . . . baby, this my quiet ritual, and I'm so glad you're joining me."

You're welcome.

If you're worried about the size of your penis, don't be. I promise it's just the right size for someone out there. Every vagina is different, just like every penis.

A friend of mine says to think of a vagina like a penis turned inside-out, then you'll realize they're all different just like you are. I've been with women who I couldn't fit in, and also with women that were like throwing a hot dog down a hallway. Don't marry either one of these - they each require a man with a penis to match their vagina, and yours ain't it. When you find that special vagina, you'll love it, and she'll love you, so just relax about it.

PS: Kegals are awesome, to the ladies who practice them: thank you!!!

- You just started doing them, didn't you?

When I was younger I was very concerned about being liked by everyone. I took it super personal if I ever got yelled at or hurt someone else's feelings.

I even had my feelings hurt when dad would say, "Don't be so sensitive!"

Here's the thing – Dad was right. Being sensitive is great, as long as you know the definition. Sensitive can mean 'connected to your emotions', which is a good thing. It can also mean 'way too worried that I won't be loved', which will screw up your life.

Emotional men are becoming more and more common these days, and the ones with masculine strength and emotional intelligence are the ones that end up with the best women.

Reminder: When someone is upset with you only 40% of it has anything to do with you. The remaining 60% is their own stuff, you just happen to be the one they're upset with at that moment. Own the 40% and don't let the rest bother you.

Note: If you overreact when someone says something you did or said bothered him or her, then they will begin to lose trust in you.

Standing strong (being present) and listening with compassion, accepting blame for any and all that you did (and not defending) is the key to being attractive and giving the other person a safe space.

One of the foundations of neuro-linguistic programing (NLP) is that our memories are snapshots in time of an event that came through our filter and is stored using whatever language we spoke at the time. This becomes our map of reality and we (incorrectly) assume that it is accurate.

When we have another event happen that's similar (or creates a similar emotion), we look at our existing map and assign meaning to the event.

In other words – your map is probably flawed, and was created by a person much younger and more naïve than you. How naïve is it then to continue to use that old map to navigate your current world?

Be the YOU that you truly are, not the you
that you *think* others want you to be.

There is no such thing as a perfect body or a perfect 10. I know we'd like to believe it's true, but it's not. Perfect 10s are for showing off to your buddies. Once the makeup is off and she's aged 20 years, you'll have to wake up next to her and have an actual conversation.

Always remember that 'future' conversation.

In other words, if you can imagine not being annoyed in 20 years by her views on life, then date her, but never, ever, ever . . . ever . . . let your visual attractiveness to her be your guide.

Everyone in life will try to give you advice, including me. If you take that advice without thinking about it first, then you're an idiot. Except for my advice...always do the shit I say to do...it makes me happy.

You're welcome.

Advice for parents: You can pick your own nose, and you can pick your own path. Once you're kid can pick his own nose, stop trying to pick it for him. Help them not to screw up, but at some point stop picking their nose and stop picking their path.

Kids...you're welcome.

Some people are gay. Deal with it, and love them for being human. Being judgmental about their life is projecting your own judgment of yourself (or your parent's judgment) onto them, which is pretty stupid when you think about it.

Racial prejudice is the same thing ^.

On this same subject, however, do realize that homophobes or racists are dealing with their own internal BS just like you and everyone else, and are probably regurgitating from their own experience. So, feel free to feel sad for them but judging them for their views is the same thing they're doing in reverse.

When someone cuts you off, flips you the bird, or displays any other kind of road rage, always remember that **you have NO IDEA what kind of day they're having**.

You can keep your peace and stay calm, or you can escalate the situation by waving hi back with your middle finger (which gives your power to them, by the way).

It's your choice, but I always feel better when I keep my peace and my power.

The phrase, "When momma ain't happy, ain't nobody happy" was created by an emasculated dickhead who decided his wife couldn't just be happy on her own and it was his responsibility to make her happy. This is bullshit.

It ain't your job to make her happy,

it's your job to be you. So, always be you, (unless you're an asshole, then pretend you're me). She'll be happy when she's happy and unhappy when she's not and it's not your job to decide for her.

You're welcome - oh, and tell her to thank me.

Sometimes weather will suck.

This is a **safe** problem to have.

When the weather sucks, imagine what the next big problem in your life would be if the weather didn't suck, then work on that.

There's a difference between a masculine man and a feminine man, and it's nothing to do with being gay. You can love girly movies and still be a thriving heterosexual man, just like you can be a woman who loves UFC and hunting animals but still likes playing hide-the-salami with a penis. Be fine with who you are, it'll make you happier.

You're welcome.

When a drunk person says shit that offends you or someone else, you're in the right to feel angry. Being drunk isn't a license to be an asshole. As a matter of fact, **there's a sliver of truth behind everything a drunk-ass says**. If you don't like what they say when they're drunk, chances are you won't like the real them (and, by the way, you can still love them for being human and not like them), since the first thing to go is the filter they have when they're sober.

My advice: stop hanging out with mean drunks and reevaluate what you want out of that particular scene.

Drama queens aren't always women. I've seen men who will create drama with the express intent (although subconscious) of having something major to worry about so they don't have to deal with their own shit deep down inside.

Don't get caught up in it, you're bigger than that.

Take time to yourself.

There's no better way to get burned out than to do everything you can for others without remembering to do stuff for yourself.

Take a bath and watch your balls (or boobs) float, go to a bar and read, go fishing, watch the game. Do whatever you need to do to be 100% for the folks that matter in your life. And don't feel guilty about it, because in reality **they need you at your best.**

You're welcome.

For young guys:

Stay the hell away from porn!

It not only won't teach you about how to be a good lover, it'll fuck up your expectations, your libido, your very brain wiring. Trust me – I know.

I'd love to write more to you on this subject, but it would take a whole book.

Just look up NoFAP on google and read your eyes off.

If you've ever had a breakup with someone you really loved, then every relationship after that you'll be settling...

UNLESS: you get to the point where you really love the shit out of yourself...then you'll never 'settle' again.

There are folks out there who say one person in each relationship is always settling and one person is always reaching (lead / follow, whatever-the-heck you want to call it). I say bullshit.

When you stop settling for less than what you really deserve, you can have it all, including nipples. Nipples are great.

We all have an intuition - a 'gut feeling' that tells us when we're screwing up. Most of us (especially men) learn to ignore that at some point in our lives. Some idiots will even say 'no...I don't have intuition' - this is why they're idiots.

Intuition is the smartest part of you. You can develop the skill of paying attention to it (start by paying attention to your body's signals, muscle tightness, gut clench, etc. for example). It'll change your life, and you don't have to wear a tiara or meditate to learn this.

In my version of spirituality, emotions are a vibrational frequency shared between people like an airborne disease. They trigger all kinds of things in our physiology (brain waves, limbic resonance, etc.)

The most powerful of these vibrations is love.

Transcending our four-dimensional space time and tying us to one another without regard to where we are on the planet, and even without regard to where we are in time. This incredibly powerful vibrational frequency of love, in my philosophy, is God, and feeling into it gives you a way to answer any conundrum in your life.

When I was younger, I used to wonder about women who've had a kid, wouldn't their vagina be looser than women who haven't had a kid?

Answer: Nope, Not. At. All. (I made sure to test a good sample of the single mom population for you to prove this, by the way).

You're welcome.

Butterflies/spark = limbic resonance. Limbic resonance, according to 'a general theory of love' is when two people's brain waves synch up in the limbic region (the primal, reptilian part of our brain), it's a magical-type connection that only happens when the grooves in your 'record' and the other person's 'record' match.

Between the ages of 3 and 7 years old, a child is programmed with their definition of love based on the brain waves in that same region of their primary caretaker. So - if your caretaker(s) had a great, truly loving and kind relationship, then you're pre-programmed for that. When you experience butterflies it's going to be healthy every time.

Conversely, the opposite is true. If your primary caretakers had a dysfunctional relationship, then unfortunately that's what you're programmed for. In that case if you base your new relationship on butterflies then you'll always (and only) feel an initial spark with people who are likewise programmed for dysfunction. Thank God you've got a triune brain, right!???

The most worthless emotion is guilt.

Credit to Kyle Cease:
When you feel guilty you end up splitting yourself into three selves.

- *The one that did the thing,*
- *the you that feels guilty about doing the thing,*
- *and the you looking at both of those people and judging them for making a mistake*

What a waste of time – and a perfect way to take you out of self-love. Sure – you did the thing, perhaps you regret it (in the "I won't do that again" sort of way) – but guilt doesn't help you or the others affected by you.

Let it go.

There's a war going on in your mind. It's a war between the part of you that demands perfection, and the part of you that loves to just be present in the moment and experience joy.

Those two sides of you need to meet, appreciate one another, and work together.

Don't deceive yourself into thinking I (or anyone you see shooting rainbows out of a unicorn's ass online) have all this shit figured out.

We're just as clueless as you.

As a matter of fact, sometimes I'm astonished as to how brilliantly well my life works out.

Positive affirmations are useless without a mindset that is actually positive. This means your emotional world needs to be sound too.

If you feel like shit you'll think like shit.

90% of the time, when I feel bad it's due to what I've been feeding my body and my mind.

"You are what you eat" – is real.

<u>But it includes what you read, listen too, and watch.</u> So, watch your diet, watch what you watch and listen too, and pay attention only to that that is good for you.

It's impossible to truly thrive without dealing with your feelings first.

So, deal with your feelings by listening to what you feel and acknowledging them as if they were a crying baby or child in need of understanding and affection.

Clear out some space in your mind for this one: <u>you can't replace a flawed map of reality until you decide to see it as flawed.</u>

My old map of reality was created at a young age - mostly by my parents. **Now imagine driving cross- country with a map that was made 20 years ago by a 12 year old.** You're gonna get lost as hell if you don't redo that map.

Guys default to a filtered thinking about women (and other guys). We have a grading system (1-10) that measures her attractiveness in comparison with how we measure our own attractiveness. We assume she has the same system.

Women do have a similar system, but it's not based on looks as much as it is for us.

Consequently, when you think you're a 6 and therefore won't be able to date an 8 or above, you're going to be wrong sometimes. My recommendation: **throw out the filter and ignore your own grade - you may well end up with an awesome girl who is also a 10**.

Oh – and if you think you're a four – go take a piss and repeat after me; You're an eight! You're an eight!

I don't do hookup sex anymore, here's why.

I've realized that there is an enormous connection between my physical body and my spiritual self.

When I do something with my physical body, my soul is involved, and I have no choice about that. So – having sex with someone I'm not truly interested in longterm, or banging her because I haven't had sex in a while and my balls ache and my right arm is sore – fucks my soul up a little bit. You see, **we're all connected** - so unless she's at my same level and we're both making a decision to inject oxytocin via sperm and orgasms - I won't ever again have a one-night-stand or even a friend with benefits.

Sorry ladies.

I'm an escape artist. When it comes to emotional pain, I've used porn, alcohol, women, drugs, adrenaline and nicotine to escape it. I learned a while back that if I avoid feeling the pain, it stays there. **You can mask it for a while, but until you face the hurt, it will always seem to have a tremendous amount of power.**

Sit in stillness the next time you feel it – **choose not to escape, at least for a while** – once pain surfaces and you let it bounce around in your head you'll find it loses it's power, and it gets less painful.

Doesn't sound like fun, I know, but **this is the most important piece on the journey to finding self-love.**

I have a theory that there is an inverse relationship between intellect later in life and attractiveness early in life.

The more attractive a person was earlier in life, the less they had to work at getting what they want, since people automatically give breaks to attractive people.

In other words, late bloomers who are hot now but weren't in high school will generally be more intelligent and more interesting than their cheerleading peers.

Going to the gym is fun for some people - not for me. I figure out shit that I like to do that takes physical exertion and I don't call it 'a workout'.

This way I can peg the fun meter and still not look like Fat Albert.

When you're about to do something that you've felt guilty about doing in the past (like, for example, having sex with an ex girlfriend), choose one of two paths.

A.) Do the thing but decide you're not going to feel guilty

or

B.) don't do the thing.

Credit to my old lead guitarist: Guys have a man/dog switch. Sometimes that switch is in the man position, and we're gentlemanly, and actually aware of what's driving our desires. Other times our switch is in the dog position (this happens to me about once a week, usually after 3 drinks). This is fine, as long as you don't assume you have no responsibility for the switch - you do. So, "keep your filter engaged 'dog' and don't do anything you'll feel guilty about later."

PS: Actions on your part while your switch was in the dog position are still your responsibility – even if you try to claim that it wasn't you 'it was your twin brother!' who did it.

I went my whole life (I'm now 43) looking in the mirror and seeing flaws. After a shit-ton of personal development I can now tell you honestly that when I look in the mirror today I think, "DAMN I'm a sexy catch!" This feels really good. You too should do this work on yourself, it's badass, and **life is too short not to love the shit out of yourself**.

Most men (80%) spend their time making decisions in their logic mode versus their feeling mode. This is due to a spike in testosterone while we're in the womb. The 'feeling mode' is estrogen-fueled, and let's most women feel spiritually connected to other people, and to God. There's one sure-fire way to connect similarly, and that's to make love to a woman connect with her at a spiritual level.

It seriously **is** like that nine-inch-nails lyric, "you get me closer to God."

PS: if you want to know whether your a logic-based testosterone driven dude or whether you're one of the lucky guys who by default has deep emotions, then take the 16 personalities test and look at your 3rd letter, a T means thinking (logic), an F means feeling (gut).[ii]

Wanna learn how to start a business, have a better relationship, or figure out how to love your shadow self?

Hire a good coach, seriously. Not that I'm opposed to traditional therapy, I just think it's slower than strategic intervention and NLP.

Note: There's no better investment to make than to invest in yourself. Think you can't afford it? Wrong – you can't afford not too.

You're welcome.

The opposite of love is not hate, it's fear.

If you feel scared in a new relationship, this is your subconscious telling you to 'watch out, you might fall in love!' Love is a thing of the heart, not the brain, yet it's still a choice. Make the choice often.

I've never regretted falling in love, no matter how badly it ended.

Note: The only regret I have in life is not loving myself fully prior to falling in love, but only from the standpoint that it hurt another beautiful soul in the process. For those I've hurt, I'm sorry, and I truly hope your time with me enhanced your journey...and your life. I love you.

Don't confuse great sex as love - that's just a result of a selfish desire to feel the effects of oxytocin in the brain (which I love, by the way).

It's fine to desire that release, just don't confuse it with love.

Want to learn how to do something well? Copy someone who already does that thing well. Sounds easy, doesn't it? It's not. You'll have to understand the mindset behind why they do what they do before you can get it right.

Yoga pants are awesome. Just sayin'.

Age doesn't matter that much. Seriously.

I use a formula of 1/2 my age plus 7 to ascertain the youngest woman I would date. Much less than that and she's TYFM (too young for me).

Here's why; I believe the world is in a high state of awakening today. If you're 15 you're feeling it, if you're 60 you're feeling it.

We're all on this journey collectively, so don't confuse your newfound awake-ness with chronological age, the number of years you've got under you have almost nothing to do with it.

You can only serve others to the level at which you serve yourself.

Likewise, you can only love others to the level at which you love yourself.

The same thing goes for forgiveness.

The same thing goes for; value, compassion, grace, honesty, and every other positive communication and emotion.

Surf. Someday...you must surf. Nowadays you can learn it behind a boat on a lake without getting board rash, and you don't have to be in awesome shape to learn it. Find someone with a boat and just do it.

You're welcome.

95% of people who can't fix things, back a trailer, jump a wake, or ride a skateboard are wrong. They're just too scared of trying and failing to spend enough time to learn it.

By the way, a lot of folks equate others seeing them fail to actually failing, which is complete bullshit.

Kind of like everything else in life, isn't it?

No one can teach you everything,
but if you pay attention,
everyone can teach you something.

Need to back a trailer? Put your hands at the bottom of the steering wheel with your thumbs facing out. Which ever way you want the trailer to go, look at your thumbs and turn the wheel that way.

You're welcome.

There's nothing sexier than
a woman who knows she's beautiful because
of who she is,
rather than because of how she looks.

I know lots of things, but **the most valuable knowledge is the knowing that at my source, in my body, is the truth**.

When I step out of my head and feel myself breathing, hurting, longing, wanting, loving, I am the truest form of me that ever existed. And I'm a sexy mother-trucker.

Do that.

Do that.

When I get in an elevator, I like to shake things up;

I wait until everyone is in, and the doors start to close and then I say: **"Hey y'all, let's take this thing to a whole 'nother level!"**

The whole concept of being 'polite' is overrated.

I remember when I was about 18 and my new girlfriend was in the house talking to mom and dad, I went to take a piss and was so happy with life and excited to get back to the conversation that I pissed with the bathroom door open (way down the hall four rooms away). My dad pulled me aside later and said "James - close the door when you pee! People can hear that!" Bless his heart but...who gives a shit?

Everybody pees, and everybody poops! Being embarrassed of being human is the most ridiculous ideology there is.
Speaking of people in categories is categorically uncool.

In reality though - we don't have a choice. **Our brains are hardwired to filter the information we receive, through language, through our experiences, through our map of reality.** It's ok to categorize but only if you know that's what you're doing. Judging someone by how the look or act is only helpful if you know with certainty that the filter comes from our mind, not from our soul.

Our soul defaults to love, our mind defaults to protecting us and judging others. Mind=ego, Soul=truth, always remember that, and you'll never regret anything.

I used to hate being sad, until I realized what yin and yang actually are.

Without hate or fear, we can't experience love, without pain, we can't experience joy, and without loss, we can't experience what it's like to actually HAVE.

Enjoy every moment, event, person, even the painful stuff, for they are shining a light for you whether they want to or not. Sometimes they're the yin, sometimes the yang, but always remember that you can't have one without the other.

Great minds talk about ideas

Average minds talk about events [or things]

Small minds discuss people

Eleanor Roosevelt

<u>This truth</u> my friends, is why I don't hang around nor participate with people who gossip.

Extending grace, love, compassion, and forgiveness to someone else is impossible until you first extend it to yourself.

On haters:

There was a study done in 1967 where four monkeys were put in a cage, and bananas were placed at the top of a ladder. Whenever a monkey reached the bananas, the researchers sprayed them with cold water. Eventually all four monkeys tried and soon learned that the one going for the banana get's sprayed by some demented researcher. So then a monkey is removed and a new one is put in, he goes for the bananas and the other three pull him back down to keep him from getting sprayed.

Eventually all four monkeys were replaced and the monkeys still wouldn't let a new one go for the bananas (even after the water hose was removed).

It's like this with haters. When you start to challenge your old ways, they're going to try and pull you back down even if they don't understand why they're doing it. (They may even think they're doing you a favor!) Just love 'em anyway.

I know a bunch of men who are tripped out by getting a massage (especially by a male masseuse), a pedicure, or other 'girly' stuff.

This is stupid and ignorant.

Screw the facade and go get yourself taken care of once in a while. You'll feel better and you'll be more attractive because of how it makes you feel.

I believe that many people are addicted to pain or drama at some level. One reason for this is that stress or pain causes a spike in the amount of endorphins in our brain.

This gives us a temporary euphoria just like a runner's high or the feeling you get when you land a new trick on your wakeboard.

The problem isn't craving this endorphin rush, **the problem is when you mess other people's peace up as a result of your search for it.**

So...Don't...Do...This.

True drama queens (or kings) are searching for one of three things.

1.) They need something in their life to focus on / worry about so they can ignore the big problems in their life.

2.) They're addicted to the temporary euphoria that comes from pain / stress-induced endorphins.

3.) They mistake attention of any kind as a sort of love, so for them, drama => attention => love.

I'm always a little saddened when I someone who views sex (or any part of it) as dirty.

Life **is** dirty - get used to it.

Once you accept that fact you'll realize that going down on your partner, sticking your tongue in another person's mouth, and eating an Oreo cookie with milk sucked from a cow, are all about the same damn thing - and just as enjoyable.

JAMES EWING

SCREW THE FAÇADE

---

www.screwthefacade.com
je@jamesewing.us
www.jamesewing.us

Join the facebook group: Screw The Façade

End Notes

[i] *If you want to know what your Thinking/Feeling score means in your relationship – hit http://jamesewing.us/tfab-test.htm.*

[ii] *Take the 16 personalities version of the Myers Briggs test online to figure out your default for thinking vs. gut.*

Made in the USA
San Bernardino, CA
27 April 2016